WHY DOES HE TREAT ME THIS WAY

What goes on in the mind of an Angry a controlling men

Anne R. Cameron

Anne R. Cameron

INTRODUCTION

O According to Sheryl Christianson, senior programs manager at My Sisters' Place, a Catholic Charities domestic abuse shelter, "people always wonder why people continue in abusive relationships." She contends that in order to comprehend the thinking of the victim in an abusive relationship, one must first comprehend the abuser's thoughts.

Christianson argued that when we ask the victim "why do they stay," we are adding to their load. Why do people abuse and what can be done to hold them accountable are questions that need to be asked.

Christianson acknowledges that there isn't a simple solution. "It's multifaceted, but power and control are at the core of it."

Inside the Mind of an Abuser

The majority of healthy people don't consider relationships the way an abuser does. Abusers frequently believe they are an extension of their victim.

They view their victim as an extension of themselves and do not want them to lead a life apart from them. To prevent their victim from leaving, seeking assistance, or forming any other relationships, they will utilize isolation or threats.

The abuser, who wants the victim to be fully reliant, will view everything that gives their victim power, such as relationships or money, as a threat.

According to Christianson, the abuser may go to extreme tactics even if they believe the victim is attempting to end the relationship.

Abusers may put the victim, drugs, alcohol, their own anger, or other things as the cause of their violent behaviour . Some even say that their actions are driven by love or protection. Ruby persisted in a toxic marriage because she believed that once her husband got sober, everything would improve. She eventually made it out.

Learned conduct

Violence, according to some experts, is a learned trait. Some people experience violence as children and pick up the behaviour . Others mature and seek out healthier relationships, rejecting the violence they witnessed as children, according to Christianson.

"Being raised in a violent home does not automatically make one violent. Many people declare as they mature, "I will never act that way.

Abusers mix loving actions with humiliating, menacing, and dominating ones. The victim is frequently confused by this and begins to doubt herself frequently. An abuser tries to make his victim doubt both her capacity to trust others and her own perceptions of reality. It's frequently an extremely challenging mental exercise mixed with "acts of love." The ultimate aim of an abuser is to have his victim submit to his authority and control.

The victim's self-esteem, confidence, and relationships begin to deteriorate as the abuser spends more time with them, making it extremely harder for the victim to exit the relationship. People frequently are unaware of the complexities of an abuser/victim relationship, which is often characterized by a protracted period of debilitating conflict rather than a single act of violence.

Anne R. Cameron

CHAPTER 1

What in a Relationship Is Too Controlling?

Every person has different wants and needs in a relationship.

Long before we met our partners, we each developed our own unique methods of doing things.

We also have beliefs, opinions, and presumptions that have developed over years of life experience.

It's only normal for us to want our mates to share our worldview once we start dating.

In truth, we occasionally make overt or covert efforts to persuade our partners that our approach is the better way.

So when does this stop being normal and start being a problem? How can we tell whether our partner is trying to dominate us instead of coerce us? To help you figure everything out, consider the following questions:

• Do you believe that if you don't do what he commands, your partner will punish you in some way?

• Do you think your partner dismisses or ignores your thoughts or opinions?

• Have you altered many of your thoughts or opinions to align with his?

Do you feel like you've lost a lot of your independence?

• Do you keep your opinions to yourself for fear of upsetting him?

• Because you're unclear of who you are and what's proper in a relationship, do you examine everything you do (in a way you didn't before)?

• Does your man treat you less like a partner and more like a child or a slave?

• Have you lost your sense of self and identity?

If "yes" was your response to any of these inquiries, your man is exerting too much control over you.

Manipulating Men Characteristics

Not all domineering males are the bulked-up macho guys that scream and yell in movies to get their way.

They could be the friendly extrovert with a solid education or the soft-spoken lad next door. They might originate from virtually any socioeconomic background.

The craving for control and the pressure to exercise that power in their personal relationships are what they share in common.

They have mastered the skill of deceiving even the most intelligent and capable women, only to expose their true selves after they have hooked her or after she has married them.

The shift can occur gradually, like a low-grade fever that develops into a virus, or it can occur suddenly and intensely, making you wonder if an alien invaded his body over night.

The initial phase is the most challenging because of the confusion and shock. He was quite kind. He showed such love. What took place? Did I cause this in some way?

The quick answer is that you didn't do anything wrong; perhaps you should have learned how to deal with a controlling man or controlling spouse in the first place and failed to recognize the early warning signals of a controlling relationship.

Why Do Men Exercise Control?

Why does the man you have treat you this way and what's going on in his head?

Men often exercise control for the following reasons:

Anxiety about feeling "out of control" • Past traumatic experiences • Insecurity and low self-esteem • Being in control of oneself now or in the past • A need to feel superior or better than someone else

Many of these arguments are understandable, but you cannot justify them. A man does not have the right to coerce and manipulate you because of past trauma or insecurities. He must take care of himself in order to be prepared for a genuine relationship.

Research shows that these men frequently struggle with mental health conditions including anxiety and depression, indicating that they may be aware on some level that their actions are damaging to the relationship.

Men who are in control frequently believe incorrectly about their role in a relationship. They believe they are entitled and that their partners owe them something.

These men lack compassion and don't value their partner's wants and emotions as highly as they do. They could be psychologically healthy or they might have narcissistic tendencies.

But despite the fact that their actions are hurting and cruel, they still think they are right because of their distorted sense of entitlement.

The precise cause of some men's drive to dominate the women in their lives is difficult to pin down. You might have to interpret the tea leaves unless your guy divulges his fragile inner world to you. Unfortunately, most domineering males aren't excellent at being vulnerable and running the danger of being frail.

CHAPTER 2

INDICATORS OF A CONTROLLING MAN

You could be unsure if you're dating a domineering man who wants to dominate you or not. Maybe you've questioned whether his actions are typical of relationship dynamics.

We all engage in controlling behaviour from time to time, but it's crucial to understand the warning signals of a controlling boyfriend or husband that indicate the conduct is ongoing.

1. **They make their demands known.**

It's unfortunate for you if they want to do something and you don't. It's unfortunate for you if you want to do something and they don't.

You will receive an earful if you try to argue or press your argument because their needs, wants, and decisions always take precedence over yours (unless they simply don't care).

They'll make fun of you, sulk, try to make you feel bad, or ignore your request. They'll make things so awful for you that you'll just give in.

Over time, you come to accept the status quo, which, regrettably, teaches the domineering man to tighten the reins.

2. **They consistently give you criticism.**

They don't like your appearance or your speech. They play practical pranks on you. They constantly spot the mistake or flaw in your accomplishments.

Around this individual, you hardly ever feel as though you are doing enough because there is always something you could be doing better.

A domineering man will frequently attempt to divert their criticism in an effort to make you appear too sensitive or whiny. Why must you make such a huge deal out of it. I merely want to support you.

You eventually come to feel always deprived and neglected.

3. They strive to keep you apart from other people.

These men try to drive a breach between you and the people you care about and who love and support you by making overt or covert disparaging remarks.

This bully wants you to depend entirely on him, so that you submit to his demands and decisions. You don't have any friends or family to lean on, so all you have is this man, and he wants you to pay close attention to what he needs.

4. They make love and affection subject to restrictions.

A manipulative man uses love as a means of control. He is aware of your need for love and affection, so he gives it to you in exchange for your cooperation.

If you don't agree to his desire for a new car, he won't declare his love for you. Because you spent the day with your sister, he refuses to have sex. Because dinner was served too late, he gives you the cold shoulder and a steely gaze.

He trains you using these techniques to make you obey him. You get a treat if you follow orders. Disobedience results in nothing or worse outcomes.

5. They excel at creating guilt.

Men who want to manipulate women frequently use guilt-tripping. Once they identify your emotional weak point, they manipulate you like a puppet.

People that are sensitive and caring don't want to feel as though they have harmed someone, especially someone they care about. They want to win back the affection of their loved one. If the guilt is justified, which it rarely is with a dominating man, then this is OK.

They will always find a way to make you feel guilty for something you didn't do or don't bear any responsibility for, and you would do anything to get rid of that guilt.

Men in positions of power have a masterful way of making you feel accountable and as though you are the only one who can set things right by carrying out his orders.

6. They snoop on you and keep an eye on you continuously.

They are curious about your whereabouts, when you'll be back, who you're texting, what you're saying, and all of your plans.

They rummage through your belongings, rummage through your pocketbook, peek at your phone, and read your email. They believe you have no right to privacy and that they have the right to know everything about you.

They're trying to figure out how you might be managing your own life. You'll be informed if they discover anything that would jeopardize their authority.

7. They are envious and possessive.

Their extreme feelings of jealousy contribute to some of their snooping and isolating activities. Their envy is attractive at first because it demonstrates how much they must love you, but it eventually becomes sinister and complicated.

They continually question your intentions and behaviour and mistake even the most benign exchanges for flirtation.

They are worried that you will go away, so they try to regulate any interactions you have with others.

8. **Your point of view is irrelevant to them.**

They will silence you or disregard you if you voice an opinion or belief. Unless you exactly repeat your controlling partner's beliefs or attitudes, nothing you say is important.

He'll try to control the conversation, cut you off, or make rude remarks about what you said. If you try to bring this up to him, he will either brush it off or turn the tables on you to make you feel bad or in the wrong.

9. **They don't show much consideration for any of your demands.**

He will come in and demand your attention if you desire some alone time. He will ignore you if you try to communicate and instead turn on the TV. He'll whine that he's hungry and needs dinner now if you're exhausted. He will tell you to calm down if you need a hug.

He rarely considers the possibility that you may have needs beyond those that go beyond meeting his requirements. If it does, he manipulates you by using your needs as a tool.

10. **You are gas lighted.**

Gas lighting is when someone tries to convince you of something you already know is false or wrong, or when they twist facts to make you doubt yourself.

When you complain about his insults or hurtful actions, he may flatly deny them or claim that you are the one who has been unpleasant. Or he might say you're crazy and just dreaming things up.

He has more control over you if he can cause you to lose your emotional and psychological equilibrium. You start to doubt your own sense of reality, right and wrong, and judgment.

11. **They exhaust you to the bone.**

Men in positions of power may employ ruthless strategies. They will continue to debate until you start to roll your eyes. They'll relentlessly press their demands upon you. They have the ability to tighten the screws of guilt until you beg for release.

The majority of dominating males have significantly more energy to carry out their antics than you do to put up with them. You eventually collapse and let them rule all the time. The controller is in the ideal situation in this instance. It's always just me.

12. **They see cruelty as affection.**

Because they feel entitled, abusive behaviour s are seen by dominating males as acceptable and even kind. Making all the choices concerning you and your lives together is something they are doing you a favor by doing because they know best.

Sayings like "You don't need to see your family because I love you more than all of them" or "You best not leave me because I love you so much I might die" are examples of what your controlling boyfriend might say.

13. **They are cunning.**

All of the manipulative actions we've outlined here are examples of controlling conduct, but men who control women frequently go above and beyond the call of duty.

He will employ strategies like making the topic about your suffering into his when a woman tries to confront a controlling abuser. Because of my father's mistreatment of me as a child, I behave in this way. If you could just comprehend how much I do for you, you wouldn't whine so much, I say.

They are experts at transforming your worries into their anguish.

14. **They refuse to accept blame.**

To shield themselves from responsibility is one of the motivations for this deception and deflection. Men with control difficulties are unwilling to take responsibility or ownership for their harmful actions.

They won't look in the mirror and admit that the problems between you are due to them. In fact, they flip the script and blame their cruel deeds and words on you. She makes it difficult to remain calm.

In their eyes, accepting responsibility entails surrendering power and recognizing they aren't entitled to any special treatment because of their actions.

15. **To others, they appear to be terrific people.**

When he is with his spouse, a controlling man could act one way, but when he is in front of his friends and family, he may act like Prince Charming. How other people view him and the two of you as a couple is also under his control.

He will display the charm and magnetism that initially drew you to him in social situations. But once you're alone with him, the novelty wears off, and he reverts to his abusive and demanding former self.

His positive traits being displayed in front of others confounds you and makes you wonder if you are the issue. He does have this side to him, so you could think you should stick with him. Unless he's with you, that is.

16. **They believe you are never sufficient.**

It started off as subliminal advice, such as "Let's work out together and drop ten pounds." "You're growing overweight, and you need to do something about it if things are going to work between us," is now downright ugly.

He has a nasty way of judging things, even the slightest things, and he is not pleased. He doesn't like how you put the dishes in the dishwasher. When he doesn't like your outfit, he lets you know. In response to minor errors, he makes sarcastic remarks.

When you are subjected to criticism and negativity on a regular basis, it can be difficult to feel loved and validated.

17. They record results.

He mostly keeps track of his accomplishments, his efforts, and the costs he has had to bear. Because he values what you bring to the relationship less, your scorecard always trails his.

He is only able to understand the costs of being in the relationship because of his narrow focus on himself and his desire to feel superior. And he's angry about it. It wouldn't be enough to continuously perform backflips around the home.

18. They make sex strange or uncomfortable.

Physical intimacy can be strange in all kinds of weird ways with your dominating man. Your particular guy can be sexy demanding but unconcerned with your emotional and sexual requirements.

Or, he can be so disconnected from emotional closeness that he just views having sex as a physical relief.

Sex can be a tool used by some abusive males to maintain power. He will withhold it or make threats to get it elsewhere if you don't make some effort to placate him. You don't feel good about whatever is going on with him, and it's playing out in the bedroom.

19. **They'll challenge your principles and objectives.**

Your partner will try to deflate whatever achievements you may be making in your personal or professional life if he has any doubts about them.

Let's imagine you want to launch your own company, but he tells you that you lack the necessary skills. Or perhaps you've just received a promotion at work, but he wants you to decline it in order to reduce the amount of time you spend there.

He might also make an effort to undermine some of the things you hold dear. He routinely makes fun of vegetarians and prepares meat-heavy dinners for them. He accuses you of being snobby or boastful if you enjoy dressing good.

I'm sincerely sorry if any of these dominating tendencies are common in your relationship and you notice them frequently. It hurts to have your goals and dreams destroyed by a domineering partner or spouse who consumes you with their poison.

CHAPTER 3

Can men who are in charge alter?

When women recognize they are in a relationship with a domineering male, these are the next two questions that frequently arise:

1. What should I do first?
2. Is he capable of evolving?

If you are not married to this person or otherwise committed (financially, with kids, etc.), the answer to question #1 is to leave right away. Run as far away from this individual as you can.

Yes, you might still adore him and believe that he is very talented if only he wouldn't display his "dark side." However, that brings up question number two, and the response is improbable.

A controlling guy needs to be extremely motivated to alter his behaviour, and if he admits to having a controlling personality, he needs to be highly motivated to sustain his new, healthy behaviours.

When a dominating man enjoys all the benefits of being in charge, why would he change?

• He gets his way on almost everything;

• He has "taught" you and your children to do as he says

• He enjoys the feeling of power that comes with control

• He is the focus of attention

• He has control over the finances.

• To friends and family who are unaware of his Dr. Jekyll/Mr. Hyde tendencies, he appears fantastic.

It's not impossible for a domineering man to change his ways and learn how to be a mature, loving partner, but it doesn't happen often and calls for substantial self-awareness and therapy.

Why wait around to figure it out if you are merely dating this person when you can break the cord and find someone who isn't controlling?

It is far more difficult to leave a marriage or a relationship with a controlling individual if there are children involved.

In addition to the rational justifications for continuing the relationship, there are many opposing emotional factors as well, such as anxiety, low self-esteem, and unhealthily strong attachment issues.

There are steps you can do to feel more empowered and less under this bully's control, regardless of whether you decide to stay in the relationship or end it.

How Can You Handle a Man Who Is In Control?

If you are currently thinking, "My partner is controlling," here are some suggestions.

• Rebuild your social and family network. Inform a few close friends and family members about your partner's situation and let them know you need their support and ear.

• If no one is available, consult a counsellor. To guide your feelings and future decisions, you'll probably need one nonetheless.

• Clearly explain your position to your partner. Sit down with your spouse and let him know how severely his actions are affecting you, unless you are concerned for your physical safety.

• Give some examples of what you mean, how the actions are affecting your relationship, and how you feel when you engage in them.

• He will undoubtedly counter or defend himself, but at least you've let him know that you're aware of his tricks. Even if he starts to become irate, make sure to maintain your composure.

• Propose couples therapy. Ask your partner whether he would be open to attending a couple's counselling session to work on your marriage during your talk.

• An effective counsellor will identify the issue right away. Unfortunately, a lot of domineering males avoid counselling because they don't want their behaviour to be known. But in reality, it's the best method to dissuade a domineering man and change his perspective.

• Even if his control issues are the main reason you want to leave, try to avoid blaming him explicitly.

• Commend good behaviour. Be quick to recognize and congratulate your partner if you notice any positive changes. You want to emphasize kind, responsible language and behaviour. The most heartfelt question your partner ever asks is "Am I controlling?"

• Keep in mind that the control is not lost just because a few people behave well. It is a positive step, but you need to notice a pattern of persistent effort and development.

• Create some fresh limits for yourself. Protect yourself from future emotional abuse from this domineering man for as long as you are still in the relationship. Although you might not be able to stop his domineering actions or remarks, you can control how you respond to them.

• Point it out to him by saying, "This is a wonderful illustration of the controlling behaviour I've been talking about. Your guilt trips won't be effective on me anymore.

• Always carry out your commitments. Don't cave in like you have in the past if your spouse is angry or tries to control you after you tell him your plans or make a decision.

• Make an effort to ignore or avoid his rubbish. If you cave, he'll realize you don't mean business and his actions will get worse.

• If you decide to go, have a strategy in place. You can come to the conclusion that the relationship can't be saved and your partner won't ever change. Watching you leave is his idea of the ultimate loss of control. Prior to quitting the relationship, create a plan outlining the steps you must do.

• Speak with an attorney, assemble a group of friends to support you, develop an exit strategy with a counsellor, consider your finances and housing arrangements, and, if you have children, make sure you have a plan for them.

Defend your rights when dealing with domineering men.

No matter what you do, don't let his domineering behaviour go unchallenged. Your mental and emotional health deteriorates as time passes.

It gets tougher to speak up for yourself and reclaim your power in the relationship as your self-esteem and confidence erode.

Your marriage or relationship deserves a love partner that values your worth and treats you equally. Your personal decisions, deeds, viewpoints, and convictions are your own.

Don't be duped by a tyrannical man who wants to maintain control over you. Identify the behaviour for what it is and take control of your conduct.

Responses to "Controlling Men: Advising Women Involved With Bullies"

1. Lynn

29th of July, 2021 at 5:16

I've been in a relationship with emotional verbal abuse for two years, and I've had enough.

He's attempting to act differently now that he realizes I'm serious about not putting up with his trash any longer.

He will need to demonstrate some sustained consistency before I ever consider getting back together. I'm still not falling for it.

He may have been bullied as a child since he now treats ladies the same way he was treated.

not any longer!

2. **Kate July 31, 2021 at 4:56 am**

You will get where you are wanted by controlling guys. When their objective is attained, they grow weary and bored. They abandon you. The abuse increases when they see you succeed and go on happily. My ex is psychopathic because he left me and realized I was happy and doing well without him. If you choose to terminate your relationship, keep in mind that controllers are difficult to let go of. Stay resilient and safe. He will despise your life when you begin living it because it is much better. Don't let him use charm to gain entry again. He won't ever change; in fact, he'll be worse than before. all the best

3. **Annie August 22, 2021 at 2:08**

For a few years now, I've recognized this dominating trait in my husband. signs of trouble when we started dating. But I still got married to him. nearly four years. Our child is 2 years old. His threats regarding custody have fully made me feel like a hostage. Before, I tried to leave but was coerced to stay. Even if he doesn't hit me, I still feel mistreated. He is vindictive, dominating, and cunning. I want to go with every ounce of my being, but there is now a small daughter to think about. She is currently the reason I'm remaining, as he threatens to give her to me if I mention being unhappy.

4. **Sofia September 11, 2021 at 11:56**

After dating for four years, I've been married to my husband for six months. Prior to being married, I was aware of the abuse and manipulation taking place, but family pressure forced me to give in and get married despite my awareness. My mother has a heart condition and is taking medication for depression right now. After one of my older brothers passed away, she developed sadness. After getting married, I made an effort to give the marriage a chance and, in my opinion, was a good wife. He told me that he will take the required steps when the time is right even though I did not want children (means he would terminate the pregnancy with meds). I should have known that it would be an abortion, but I was stupid for not noticing. I then tried to convince him to take precautions, but he ignored me. And in just one month, I got pregnant. When I asked for medication, he gave me the excuse that the medications had side effects and would make it difficult for me to conceive in the future. He also pointed out that I live in a conservative society where family planning is unethical and that I was wrong for being determined to abort my child. In this class, I was anxious and disturbed and did not feel like engaging in any physical intimacy. However, he repeatedly forced me to do so, and one night when I was attempting to avoid being touched, he overdosed on medication while I was asleep and woke me up to tell me, ruining my sleep. The following morning, I was so stressed out by everything, I tried to take an overdose of medication to get rid of it all. He hit me to try to stop me, and as the argument progressed, he became abusive, accusing me of killing my brother and doing everything else that could harm me. But once more, his actions were justifiable because he made every effort to stop me from trying to kill myself, and once more, it was my fault for instigating the assault. I had only been married for 1.5 months when this all occurred. My parents don't like it when he hits me, but they don't seem to care because it was only one time. But right now, I have no feelings for him whatsoever. It was difficult to break free of this throughout these five months since I had to consider the future of the baby and society's expectations. I tried to be a little bit good to him for my own peace of mind. But the moment I try to be polite to him, He becomes demanding once more, and I back off. Now that I'm experiencing pregnancy discomfort, I'm at my mother's house, where he is being nice and good except for complaining that I don't love him. I do not, but he believes that since I am his wife, I should love him. However, now that I can't, I don't feel it anymore, and he accuses me, which causes me stress even though he claims I'm interested in someone else. He claims that even when I satisfy his demands, it is useless because I don't feel love.

However, I believe I am carrying out my responsibility. He also begs for my forgiveness for the past, hoping that it won't be such a big problem that I can't forget and forgive, but my heart won't let me love him or forgive him. In fact, I'm worried that if I give him another chance, he'll injure him and start manipulating again. He attempts to influence me into loving and forgiving him, and the lengthy conversations only make things worse for me.

I've been expecting for more than five months, and I'm worried that all this worry may have an adverse effect on my unborn child. Sometimes I even feel bad for stressing myself out and putting my baby's health at jeopardy. My mother advises me to follow his wishes if he apologizes, but I doubt there is much likelihood that he will have changed. His claims are not reliable. I don't want to trust him again and end up feeling foolish.

I have to stay with him, but I can't think about it since it would make my heart suffer worse. In addition, if I get what I expect rather than what I don't expect, there will be some relief, but stress will still exist because of his pressure to forget and forgive.

I'm not sure whether to give him a chance or just let things go.

5. **Damaged**

17th of March, 2021, at 1:04

Now, I visit a counsellor. He nearly got me killed. He was arrested after I phoned the police. He had a good attorney, and the only accusation was harassment.

He hurt me physically and verbally to the point where I am unable to work.

My therapist claimed that he has never loved me and is a narcissist.

I dated him for 10 months after falling in love with him. First, he emotionally and physically assaulted me for six months before he tried to kill me when I went to his place to end our relationship. I considered him to be my true love.

6. **Catherine Lundquist**

18 April 2021 at 8:26

This was how my first husband was, and he would not alter. It didn't take him very long to start physically abusing me. The abuse was sparked by anything I did or said, not even how I looked. One day, while he was at work, I had someone take me out of the house and take me somewhere safe. He attempted to convince my family to force me to return to him so he could murder me. He was never allowed to come close to me again.

7. Kelly

April 28, 2021, 1:51

As I sit here, my mouth is hanging open. For the past two years, every word of this has been my life. When I had had enough, I departed two weeks ago. The only term I could use to describe what was happening was "bully". Right now, I'm a mess. It's terrible to play these mental games for that long. I'm not even sure how to cure myself. For this, I'm grateful. At least I am certain that leaving was the right decision. It was nice when he was doing well. before ceasing to be.

8. Mary

14th of June, 3:58 PM

now 25 years. He really is excellent when he's at his best, it's true! But he blows really high when he is furious, exhausted, annoyed, or anxious. I feel as though I spend every minute of every day walking on glass eggshells. He repeatedly makes demeaning charges, which really hurts, and he occasionally acts violently by spitting, pushing, and shoving people. He has only ACTUALLY struck me once, but he has physically intimidated me a great deal more frequently. He throws things at me and breaks stuff out of rage. I think I may be that horrible because of how he makes me feel about myself. He's always right and I'm always wrong because I don't listen, don't act in a "proper" way, and don't "trust" him. Favorite phrases include "If you'd just LISTEN," "You never pay ATTENTION," "That's why you don't have any friends," and "If you'd make more money to pay for xxxx then I wouldn't get so furious!" continuing forever. I fear living out my life.

9. **Lady L**

24th of July, 2021, 12:06

I like to consider myself to be a strong female with a head. I do, however, have a three-year relationship with my partner. Even with all the warning signs flying around, it can be difficult to avoid being drawn in. He was incredibly nice and reliable at the beginning! He seemed like an overly protective man to me. not just with me but also with himself. I mention this because after our six-month honeymoon phase, I began to wonder and ask him why he hadn't taken me to this property he rents, but instead chose to pay for hotels, and it took him three years to allow me to go to his place. I warned him repeatedly to leave me alone and charged him with leading a second life. He would revert to calling me materialistic rather than protecting my emotions. I ignored the advice to flee from all of my close friends and family members. After being with him for three years, he eventually invited me over to his apartment when I finally broke up with him. Sadly, I was drawn in once more, but this time it was far worse. Since the first time I met him, my instinct has always advised me to go, yet three years later, I'm still terribly miserable. Fortunately, I was well aware of these difficulties, but what's tragic is that I decided to stay. The article struck every single point on the head. He made an effort to manage whatever I did. I couldn't go to the supermarket, the gym, or anywhere else without him making an absurd accusation. I continually question my worth while trying to find reasons to continue. I've always known it was my choice to stay, but I can't help but blame society for the psychological effects it has on women over 35 who are childless and single. I have felt the effects of desperation being around an ing male. As a result, I once again discovered the value of calm and the need to always trust your gut.

Sarah, 10.

26th of July, 7:55 PM

Everything that has been written is what he did to me during our two years of marriage. He got so sceptical and apprehensive of me that it was best for him to separate, thus it was fortunate that he was the one who sought a divorce. But because of his actions, I developed depression and made repeated attempts to take my own life.

Such men will never understand the value of a real lady. However, I firmly believe in both God and karma. Everyone is visible. He has complete vision. Justice will be served for the suffering. Simply wait and observe.

11. **Trish**

29th of July, 2021 at 4:53

Reading about other people's experiences is quite helpful. I do appreciate you sharing them, everyone. When you find yourself in a difficult position and are unsure of what is real and whether you are dreaming, you need an article that is clear and doesn't pull any punches... There are numerous instances of extreme seriousness described here. I pray to God that you all survive them and enjoy the rest of your lives.

In contrast to the majority of your experiences, my issue is still in its infancy, but I have noticed that many of you have 'sensed' big problems early on yet continued into a more intricate, deeper, hell mouth of a relationship. I understand! I'm currently at the point where I'm attempting to stop myself from going any further. John and I have been together for a year. No matter how much effort or what my intentions are, there isn't much I do that he finds admirable. However, there are many comments about what I do wrong, including comments about my eating habits, friendships, how I spend my time, how I treat my dogs, and how I drive. He also claims that anyone would understand why the other person has trouble with me, but he would never support me if I needed it. In front of his buddies, he has criticized me for the silliest of things. As you might guess, when I confront him about it, he pushes back, and I only learn more reasons why he felt compelled to do it. I am financially independent, have a strong support system of female friends, and I live on my own. I have NO EXCUSES. However, I am still a part of the union. I am aware that it cannot continue. I know I have to go. Good luck to me. He is the one on the phone. However, he only wants to communicate if it's "fluffy" and not if I want to resolve a problem.

I believe there is a basic weakness or limitation in my psychological makeup that causes me to get drawn into these circumstances, therefore after I deal with the immediate problem, i.e., get myself out of this situation, I need to look much further into how to prevent it from happening again.

I sincerely hope the people whose stories I've read have been able to flee. Those of you who have probably wondered what the heck took you so long after dealing with all the awful worry and self-doubt.

August 4, 2021 at 10:48 a.m.

It's high time ladies understood that ALL males are just like this. Although not all males physically abuse women, all of them want to control them because they believe they are superior to them. Have your own property and start off protecting yourself, ladies. Have a lawyer on hand from day one, no joint assets, and no shared finances. PROTECT. PRESERVE, PRESERVE

@ 12:44 a.m. on August 6, 2021

As a victim of domestic violence, I did leave. I had to escape because the monster was threatening to hurt my 10-month-old daughter. No matter where a woman goes, if she is not being abused, it is preferable for her child to reside there if you have to live in your car.

14. drained and weary

24th of August, 2021 at 5:37

It started out far away. He requested that I provide him screenshots of my conversations. He wants me and my two kids to move in with him. I made a custody change request. While pretending to be my family, he called the court. I am CONSTANTLY being accused of cheating. I was so over it that I left without telling him. He continues to ask for access to my phone and emails six months later despite my arguments that I should be released if I have nothing to conceal. Finally, I informed him that enough was enough. I no longer have any contact with him, and I'm getting my phone back. He changed. Although it's not physically possible, my brain is so jumbled that I can't even enjoy a glass of wine without checking in. I don't cheat, and I love him. He advised me to establish my worth. demonstrate my deserving of his affection. Just trying to go about my daily business. What do you think, guys? I don't have any friends or a Facebook account, therefore I don't have anyone to talk to. More than two years have passed since I last felt at ease.

15. **Adam**

28 January 2020, 8:07 p.m.

I stand in solidarity with any PERSON who has experienced any form of controlling or abusive behaviour because I was in an emotionally abusive relationship. It forces you to consider your morality and can set off a terrible downward spiral of self-pity, melancholy, and loneliness. However, I take issue with the overtly sexist and targeted argument against men, even when the reasons expressed resonate with me on such a personal level. It is important to note that women are equally likely as males to exhibit these characteristics so that anyone in need of support—regardless of what is between their legs—can get unbiased assistance.

CHAPTER 4

LOVE TO ALL OF YOU!

Why is he treating me in this manner?

Have you ever questioned your boyfriend's treatment of you, acting as though you are unimportant to him?

When you realize that's not how someone handles someone they care about, do you feel hurt?

Emotional abuse can hurt a lot and leave you feeling hopeless, but physical violence is one thing. Negative interactions and poor treatment are particularly hazardous to your health when you're in an emotionally abusive relationship.

Why is he treating me in this manner?

It may be challenging to identify the signs of emotional abuse or understand why they are happening. These interactions make you doubt yourself and wonder what you each say and do, leaving you muttering to yourself, "It wasn't always this way, was it? " This is incredibly unsettling.

Why is he treating me in this manner? No, things weren't always this way. and that's why it's so hazardous. Most likely, your partner occasionally treats you well. Now when you're further along in the relationship and your emotions are out in the open, he's changed.

He may not be as available as he previously was (without a valid reason), or he may be emotionally distant without cause, or he may start arguments and conflicts, withhold affection, stop showing you thoughtfulness, or just stop caring about you.

You are left with some dreadful, damaging questions as a result of all of this. "Where did I go wrong? What's wrong with me? What did I do that caused him to reconsider? Why is he treating me in this manner?

the truth-check You didn't attempt to influence him to do otherwise. Without a weapon—either physical or emotional—no one has the ability to make someone do anything they don't want to. A man intentionally chooses to treat you poorly when he does so.

Not only does he choose it, but you also permit and support it. In essence, you give individuals permission to act in a way toward you that enables them to get away with it.

When you put up with someone's poor behaviour or subpar efforts, you are essentially saying to them, "This is okay with me. Or, at the very least, I won't disturb you too much. You may go ahead.

Why is he treating me in this manner? Unfortunately, despite being truthful, this explanation falls short of providing a complete or genuine explanation of this particular pattern of behaviour , which is in fact a type of domestic violence.

People are frequently mistreated because, first, they receive the love they desire and tolerate poor behaviour the rest of the time in exchange for the scraps of love they hope to someday receive, and second, because their self-esteem is so low that they feel (consciously or unconsciously) that this is what they deserve.

Why is he treating me in this manner? If you put up with unfair treatment, you're communicating to your partner that you don't value yourself. You show him that you think his cruel treatment of you is all you deserve. And each time you give him a second chance, you are encouraging his terrible behaviour .

Why does he still treat me badly?

Why does he still treat me badly? There are various causes for a man to start abusing you. Whether or whether something had happened before he suddenly changed his attitude toward you would depend on the circumstances. It is impossible for someone who has shown such compassion to change without a valid reason.

first, ask yourself. The majority of us can wonder, "Why does he keep mistreating me? " Did you understand your question was the incorrect one?

Remind yourself that it is not your fault if you receive unfair treatment. The person that treats you unfairly is the one who is doing improperly in their words, actions, or intentions. Don't worry about it; it's not your fault.

If you let this go on, it will be your fault. Therefore, consider why you are tolerating your partner's abuse.

Even if you wouldn't put up with the same behaviour in other people, you keep giving your lover the benefit of the doubt in the hopes that he will change.

Here are a few justifications for why he keeps treating you badly.

• He's done it previously and avoided major consequences. He thinks that since there are no consequences for his actions, he may act recklessly and get away with it.

• You don't voice your concerns about his recent behaviour : If you don't let him know how you feel, he might assume you approve, which is unhealthy for the relationship.

• You fear losing him if you voice your displeasure: You should be free to communicate your sentiments to your partner in a relationship without fear of losing him. You might want to re-evaluate your relationship with him if you are unable to accomplish it. It's a relationship, not a dictatorship!

• Unresolved issues: Not all guys voice their opinions. Many men have a propensity for passive-aggression and emotion-based behaviour. For instance, he might become furious if he heard something bad about you.

You can start to wonder why he keeps acting in this way since he may not want to come clean and tell you what's wrong, he may come off as cold and emotionally unavailable, and he may not want to open up to you.

• He's having problems: It's likely that your partner is going through problems that you aren't yet aware of.

He has a great tendency to project his fury, perplexity, and despair onto you in circumstances like this. If you have any suspicions that this might be the case, try to have a heart-to-heart conversation with him.

• He's tired of the relationship: Men may find it difficult to explain their desire to break up with someone or their lack of affection. In an effort to break you apart from the connection, they mistreat you.

How do you know if your partner is abusing you?

There is no manual to consult while resolving relationship problems. How can you tell if you're not entirely that when your spouse is trying to refute you?

But if you're credulous, When he tells you that you are acting theatrically, you won't know what to do, and you'll start to doubt yourself and feel confused since you think you have a good reason to be angry with him.

You think he's been a lousy spouse, but he insists that he's just going through a rough patch. What are your core convictions, then?

Have you ever questioned how to recognize whether your lover is treating you unfairly? These indications will relieve any residual worries you may have about how he has been treating you.

Being mistreated is one thing; abuse is quite another. It merely means that he isn't exerting himself sufficiently. Inform him that if he doesn't get his act together, he will lose you.

• He doesn't put you first:

His buddies used to gripe that they didn't get to see him all that often when you two first started dating. To be honest, he currently appears to be living the single life.

He has a busy social calendar, a tough job, and he certainly needs to exercise at the gym. What do you do then to find the time? You are at the bottom of his priority list. And no matter what he says, that is false.

• You haven't recently participated in an exciting activity:

You've started to secretly like your friends' company more than his because of his terrible organizational skills.

Instead of eating dinner at the same spot every night, you would prefer to remain home and relax. He has given up trying to keep the flame alive.

• When you try to talk things out with him, he becomes combative:

When you try to discuss a matter with him, he responds so angrily that it appears as though you are questioning both his integrity and his very existence. If his ego was a bit smaller, his mind could be less obscured and more receptive to seeing things from your perspective.

• He regularly discounts your viewpoints:

Everyone wants a guy who values our thoughts and believes in our abilities.

How do you know if your partner is abusing you? If he does this, it is an obvious sign that he is not treating you well.

Do you understand how it feels when you clearly tell your partner anything and he still affirms it to others? Or does he make you look bad in front of others? or he starts lecturing you when you try to speak up!

• You experience exclusion when you attend a social event:

When your boyfriend's friends come over, you all have a good time. since you've been rather close to his wonderful buddies. Although you don't anticipate him to constantly be at your side, you do anticipate him to be aware of you.

You want him to look at you, sit next to you for a while, maybe even tease you. Without making a huge announcement or doing too much, it should be clear to anyone close that the two of you are dating. Why does he treat me this way? you might wonder when someone ignores you in front of others.

• He claims that your emotional outbursts are excessive.

You can't say I'm being too dramatic up until you accuse me of crying because you ate my pizza. It would be best if you stayed away from it even then. He probably hasn't had much experience with women if he constantly refers to your feelings as "dramas."

He does not respect your time:

He keeps you waiting and anticipates that you will be available for unforeseen circumstances (as per his convenience.) The majority of your interactions will occur once he has scheduled ALL of his other engagements and is free.

On the other hand, you have to abandon your goals and opt for him instead of waxing. If you don't like it, let him know that you're busy and he may make plans that fit your schedule.

• He conceals several things:

And most of these secrets are connected to certain women. On occasion, he might phone them, text them, or engage in conversation with them on social media. He rejects the subject or avoids talking about these girls even if you ask him who they are or how he knows them.

• No matter how you feel about it, he still communicates with his ex:

Despite having no justification, does your partner maintain touch with his ex-girlfriend?

He feels that even if they don't collaborate or hang out as pals in a group, they are great buddies.

Unexpectedly, whenever he visits his ex, he doesn't seem too enthusiastic on you joining them. Despite being aware of your emotions, they still meet. Are they not just friends?

• Your family or friends don't get along with him:

A guy who is sincere about you will always make an effort to win over your loved ones and obtain their support for your decision. Contrarily, your pals think he's a bad guy.

It's easy to let your emotions get the best of you when you're in love. Good friends, however, can foresee a breakup months or even years in advance. So, pay heed to what your reliable friends have to say.

When you tell them about your boyfriend, pay attention to the conversation to see if they make any overt declarations about how awful a boyfriend he is.

CHAPITER 5

What can you do to improve how your partner treats you?

What can you do to improve how your partner treats you? Do you have the impression that, despite your best efforts to win his favour, your lover no longer considers you to be a priority? Do you feel like you're going crazy and that he thinks more highly of his friends and other ladies than you?

You no longer need to worry because, dare I say it, you can make your partner treat you nicely. If you apply your brains and a few tried-and-true methods, you can force him to give you what you deserve.

You shouldn't settle for someone who disregards you and treats you like a mere option when it comes to love. You are entitled to much more than this. You require a companion who will not only call you when they are having a problem.

Here are some suggestions on how to get better treatment from your partner.

• Hold your own opinions: If you want your spouse to treat you fairly, you must be adamant about your viewpoints.

You can't just accept what your boyfriend wants if it makes you uncomfortable. It's not always a negative thing to hold a different perspective. It simply suggests that you have a set of views that you consistently uphold and that you use your intellect while making decisions.

If a man notices that you hold beliefs that are different from his, he will be more intrigued by you. He will be curious about you and find you to be a mystery. He will be interested to learn what drives you and what makes you lose control.

If you carry yourself in this manner, no man will ever find you boring and you and your partner will always have something to discuss. Isn't it true that sticking to your principles pays off?

• Refuse to accept anything less than the best. How do you get your lover to treat you better? is addressed in this very helpful article. Many females just accept whatever occurs in their romantic relationships.

They lack the self-assurance to follow their rules, work hard for themselves, and pursue their happiness because they think they were lucky to find a man. You should be aware that this is a bad plan of action. If you don't put in the effort, the fairy tale won't come true. If you don't earn a man's respect and good treatment, you can't expect him to.

Consequently, you should never settle for anything less than your entire potential. Do not simply assert that everything is good and that there have been worse relationships. NO! If you have this mind-set, you will never be content.

You will never receive the care you need. The most essential thing is that you will never receive the love you deserve. Keep in mind that if you stand up for your rights early on in the relationship, you'll be able to appreciate it later.

• Take emotional action. Sometimes words are not as powerful as deeds. If you feel that you are being taken advantage of and you have previously told him about it, act on your feelings. Usually, just telling him how you feel won't be enough.

Show that he is not attempting to elevate your status in his eyes. To make him hunger for you, try placing some space between the two of you. Don't spend too much time wondering "Why does he treat me this way?" Try this strategy out.

• Let him practice compromising. If you decide to go on a date with him, don't merely agree to a time that works for him. You ought to be able to hang out and go on dates on days when neither of your schedules is full.

Let him know that you two need to develop a sense of compromise. It shouldn't only be you who needs to change; you deserve better than what he's providing you.

• Be equipped to handle the worst-case scenario. When the ultimatum finally comes, nothing has changed. Get ready for the worst-case scenario— that the relationship will end.

Although I think we all deserve a chance at success, I don't think it's fair to keep presenting you with the same challenge. You are a human being who deserves to be cherished and adored. Never allow one individual to ruin your reputation.

• Don't do anything that will make your lover treat you poorly: Sometimes you can be the cause of your own bad behaviour . Pay attention to how you handle your connection. Due to the way you act, you can be the one who is toxic in your relationship.

· Constantly strive to improve yourself. Never stop striving to be your best. Never be content with what you currently have. The best way to get people to love you more is sometimes to love yourself.

• Be open and truthful about your preferences. Don't presume that your significant other knows what you want from the relationship. You must be able to effectively articulate your desires if you want them to change.

• Exemplify for him. I wish he would spend more time with me or that we could spice up our love relationship, women regularly tell us. I imagine that he has the same thought.

And even if we value men taking the initiative in some situations, empower yourself and demonstrate how to do it.

If you and he are both always working, invite him unexpectedly to a romantic lunch at your house or greet him at the door with an embrace and kiss. Tell him afterwards how joyful it makes you feel and how much you can't wait to do it again.

Why do I continue to be with someone who mistreats me? The most frustrating thing is when we can't let go of our affection for someone who treats us badly. Why do we struggle so much to end relationships that we are aware aren't working? Why can't we just end our relationship if we know it's for the best?

Regardless of whether we want to or not, breaking up with someone is never simple. We have such high hopes going into relationships that ending them might feel like the end of a dream. Or perhaps a nightmare is coming to an end.

Why do I continue to be with someone who mistreats me? Fear is one of the most fundamental motives for sticking with unsuitable partners. It's simple to think that nothing will work out if this doesn't. They therefore stay with a less than ideal partner in order to avoid loneliness. People who feared being alone more were more willing to put up with a subpar relationship.

And while though we often stereotype guys as being marriage- or commitment-phobic, it turns out that they are as terrified of living alone forever. The fear of being alone drove both men and women. The fear of dating again may also be terrible after breaking up with a horrible partner, in addition to the anxiety of being alone.

Some people may experience depression when dating. Instead of starting over, we'd prefer to suffer in silence in a partnership that offers company. It's not acceptable to have to maintain a relationship despite wondering, "Why does he treat me this way?"

Everyone finds dating to be challenging. You'll have to cope with odd small talk, sometimes unpleasant or even frightening characters, and that one person who will go out of his way to call you awkward and repulsive if you reject him.

There is a lot of dread when you mix the turmoil of dating with the terrible thought of being by yourself. Couples that ought to have split up a long time ago are kept together by this dread.

Why do I stay with someone who treats me poorly, you might be asking yourself. You stick around him in the hopes that he'll change. Many people, especially women, hold out hope and confidence that they can alter the characteristics of their partner that give them the most grief.

Maybe your husband doesn't spend enough time with you and spends too much time with his friends. He might be constantly at work and pay special attention to you. She might not treat her family with the respect you would like. You could wish she felt better about herself.

You really believe that if you love them enough and don't give up on them, they will change?

Many people who are unhappy in relationships but are unable to end things with their partner do so because they believe they can make things right between them and subsequently lead fulfilling lives.

You will undoubtedly be unhappy if you do not end your connection with your partner unless you are content with who they are right now. People are irreparably broken. No matter how hard you try, you won't be able to alter them; they can choose to change on their own.

invested time? Despite the fact that you've spent a lot of time with this person, don't waste any more time with them. Cut the bait right now, take care of yourself for the next few minutes, hours, and days, and put all your attention into finding the person of your dreams.

In addition, I believe that no matter how our interactions with others turn out, they are never a waste of time. You discover a lot about yourself and your relationships by spending time with someone.

That time will only be lost if you leave without applying what you've learnt. Therefore, resist the temptation to prolong a relationship that you know should end just because you have already put time in it.

CHAPTER 6

Signs

Signs that he mistreats you

signs that he mistreats you. We sometimes work harder to make an impression on strangers than on people who are closest to us. Additionally, keep in mind not to take your closest friend or relative for granted.

Nobody likes to think that their partner is treating them poorly. Sometimes we don't realize we're being mistreated until it's too late. On the other hand, those close to us regularly pay attention to what is happening. It's possible that your friends and family have made an effort to discuss this with you. Accepting the circumstance is challenging.

There are several telling signs to look for when someone we care about behaves us poorly. If you recognize the signs, you'll be able to cease the harsh treatment or find a method to end the relationship completely. No one deserves anything less than complete respect and affection when it comes to personal relationships.

• If your companion exhibits excessive behaviour : Have you told your partner that there are some things they should avoid doing around or to you because they make you uncomfortable? Many of us have probably had similar discussions.

Most adult couples do this! On the other side, if your partner consistently transgresses your limits regarding things you'd prefer not to happen, that is one of the Signs he treats you unfairly.

Your partner should always abide by your established boundaries, which should be crystal obvious. If this happens, it's crucial to sit down with your spouse and have a meaningful discussion about your boundaries and how you feel when they are crossed. It's time to move on and find someone who can respect your boundaries if they are unable of doing so.

• He disrespects you: You may be dealing with a partner who doesn't respect you if they constantly talk over you or make fun of you in ways that you don't enjoy. The way your partner is acting passively antagonistic toward you is another sign that they don't respect you.

• He only calls you when he needs your help: The number one sign that he is treating you as an alternative is if he only calls you when he needs your help. He won't even make an effort to be there in person for you.

Instead, he will call and get in touch with you every few days for a few days, then he will vanish for a few weeks and then come back. And anytime he does get in touch with you, it's always to ask you for something.

So, if you see this warning sign, turn around and go the other way. A man who values you will want to bond with you and show his love for you. You don't need to disappear like this in your life.

• He Constantly Lies: Lying hurts, and we all hate liars. Lying simply serves to exacerbate a peaceful connection, and a healthy relationship cannot exist if one party is lying all the time.

He need not fabricate important details; he might make up insignificant ones instead, including his whereabouts and current activities. This is a major red flag in any relationship, and while white lies might be overlooked, blatant and unnecessary deceptions aren't required for a healthy connection. If he feels the need to lie to you, you need to wake up and realize that he is not the one for you.

• He doesn't fully integrate you into his life: Aside from the fact that he's lying to you, your partner is uncomfortable with the idea of fully integrating you into his life. You've let yourself be vulnerable to him, but you don't know where he lives or have ever met his family.

People act in this way because they have the option to do so. Why would he spend time and energy getting to know you or letting you get to know him if you aren't a constant in his life and are easily replaceable? Watch for information about his private life that isn't consistent. This situation has raised another red flag.

• He makes threats to break up with you: This is one of the many tell-tale signs that he mistreats you. The worst threats to your mental health are those that come from someone who pretends to love you. Manipulators are skilled at controlling their prey.

He knows that you love and care about him, and if he is only considering you as a choice, he will take advantage of that. Another warning sign is if he makes threats to end things with you but doesn't follow through. He only wants to use you, therefore it's probably best if you end your relationship with him now before he uses it against you later.

Why does he treat me like this?

Why does he treat me like this? He treats you badly because he lacks empathy, is inconsiderate, and cares nothing about you. Just enough of him is charming to keep you intrigued. Manipulation is what this is, and it is nasty and dishonest.

He doesn't seem to be that interesting. Even if the relationship is only sex and has no other obligations, who wants to spend ANY time with a horrible person?

Why does he treat me like this? Everyone has been poisoned by someone who sprayed their poison on us. At times, it feels more like soaking. We've all had (or have) at least one difficult person in our life who makes us twist over ourselves like barbed wire in an effort to satisfy them—only to never fully achieve. Difficult individuals gravitate toward the reasonable.

Their subtlety and capacity to elicit the conventional response, "It's not them, it's me," are what cause such sorrow. You could start to question your "oversensitivity," "tendency to misunderstand," and other characteristics. Chances are, it's not you if you consistently suffer harm or if you constantly alter your behaviour to prevent harm.

Why does he treat me like this? Here are a few responses to your query.

• He is merely evil and unconcerned with your feelings.

• He is trying to find a means to end the union.

• He is projecting his own troubles onto you because he is preoccupied.

• He lacks self-confidence, therefore the way he treats you makes him feel superior.

• He is seeing another person.

He had a lot of horrible experiences growing up, so it doesn't seem improper to him. He is also being influenced by some nasty pals.

He's envious of you or thinks you're cheating. You're fighting.

He treated me as if I had no value.

He treated me as though I were unimportant.

No matter how strong and self-assured you are, when you're single and dating, you meet all kinds of awful individuals who can't comprehend how gorgeous you are and how fortunate they are to have a chance at being a part of your life.

You don't have to put up with a man who views you as secondary to other options rather than his top choice. You must not. If he doesn't treat you like a priority, treat him as follows.

Give him a deadline if his actions make you feel like "He treated me like I was nothing."

Even though it could be uncomfortable, doing this is the greatest thing you can in this circumstance for yourself. As long as he doesn't start acting like your lover, tell him you're not interested. If you're concerned, remember that defending your rights makes you a hero to all women.

Pass on. Maintaining your composure and standing up for yourself won't help if you second-guess your actions and wonder whether you ought to have done something different. Don't look back after taking a step back. You may want to let him go if he isn't going to treat you like the wonderful girlfriend you deserve. I'm aware that it won't be simple.

A man who doesn't respect you won't ever be a good companion. You shouldn't waste your time trying to influence him or tolerating his actions. Instead, go because you are better off alone than with someone who doesn't value you and doesn't treat you as such.

He treated me as though I were unimportant. If he acts as though you are unimportant to him. Because you love him so much and are confused by why, you sometimes even cry in the shower or at night. I believe it would be best if you took a break from the relationship. Consider viewing everything from the perspective of an outsider. If he doesn't cherish you, there are a thousand other men who will. Take some time to yourself and relax. If you've been asking yourself, "Why does he treat me this way?," it's conceivable that he doesn't feel very good about you.

How he treats you reflects his feelings for you.

How he treats you reflects his feelings for you. It's no secret that his behaviour toward you is an indication of how he feels about you. preferably when they are adults. If he treats you poorly, keep in mind that his behaviour is a reflection of his feelings for you. Sadly, we still play heart tricks on one other as adults, and the more times you fall for it, the more times you'll be duped.

However, there are times when what seems like "coyness" is actually a signal. You can tell a man values you if he treats you with respect. A guy is treating you poorly if he makes you feel awful.

Name-calling, mockery, and outright flaking are not signs of a man who treats you well in a relationship. That behaviour is completely inappropriate. You deserve to be treated like the queen you are, even when it's difficult to put yourself out there for love.

How he treats you reflects his feelings for you. It's likely that a man will think poorly of you if he treats you poorly. If they treat you poorly, it's not because they're trying to be difficult or keep you under control; rather, it's because they don't like you or, worse yet, don't respect you.

Any relationship expert will tell you that one of the most important parts of a partnership is communication. The objective is that the relationship has matured to the point where you can ask how things are doing without it turning into a shouting match or silence.

The objective is that the relationship is mature enough for you to be able to ask how things are doing without it turning into a shouting match or silence.

The way someone treats you is a clue as to how they feel about themselves on a deeper level. When someone makes a negative or constructive statement about us, we may unavoidably take it personally. Recognize that people can observe and voice their opinions, so put your attention instead on developing a two-way relationship.

How he treats you reflects his feelings for you. Even if they can't express themselves well, some people will treat you like a queen and think the world of you. However, the opposite can (and frequently does) happen, and it is your responsibility to recognize the signs and respond appropriately.

He most likely doesn't care if he ignores your advice. If he speaks over you, he thinks his opinion is more important than yours. If he treats you disrespectfully, he doesn't respect you.

Conclusion: I wonder why my partner treats me so poorly. You're coming to understand how crucial it is to live independently. Never allow anyone to treat you poorly. It doesn't matter if the person is your boss, a co-worker, a member of your family, or even your partner.

If someone you care about treats you badly, you must step in. Recognize the issue and start setting constraints. You have to end this unhealthy relationship if everything else fails.

Conclusion: I wonder why my partner treats me so poorly. Knowing what to do when someone treats you badly will help you feel more assured about who you are and what you deserve.

Accepting Reality

Young People Inquire.

Why Does He Handle Me Like That?

"[My partner] frequently makes ridiculous accusations against me. But I can't get away from him emotionally. —Kathri

"You couldn't see [any wounds] on the outside, but it ached so much inside."

—Andrea, who received a punch from her lover.

AN ALL-TOO-COMMON occurrence A young woman is dating a guy who seems like the epitome of charm and politeness. But over time, he starts to transform. Replaced with sharp sarcasm and demeaning criticism are words of affection. She initially dismisses it all as crude but kind teasing. However, the situation worsens into a recurrent pattern of verbal abuse, angry outbursts, and declarations of extreme regret. The young woman suffers in quiet, hoping that things will improve because she feels some way accountable for the inappropriate behaviour . They don't, though. Now her guy starts screaming and shouting. In one episode of wrath, he even shoves her hard! She worries that he may strike her again soon

An unrelenting bombardment of criticism, cruel comments, and wrath may be directed towards young men and women who are involved in romantic relationships that involve physical or verbal abuse. Are you experiencing this? (See "Some Warning Signs" box.) If this is the case, you could feel so helpless and ashamed that you simply do not know what to do.

Situations like these don't happen as frequently as you may believe. According to research, one in five people had been the victim of dating violence. This estimate increases to four out of five when verbal abuse is taken into account as a type of violence. Not all victims are women, despite popular belief. Nearly equal percentages of men and women, according to a British study on dating violence, reported having victimizing partners.

Why does misbehaviour like this happen during courtship? If you find yourself in such a circumstance, what should you do?

God's Viewpoint

You must first comprehend the gravity of God's position in this matter. It is true that those with flaws are more likely to say and do things that hurt other people. (James 3:2) It's also true that even those who adore and respect one another can disagree on occasion. For instance, Barnabas and the apostle Paul were seasoned Christians. However, they did once experience "a sudden rush of rage." (Acts 15:39) Therefore, if you're dating someone, there can occasionally be some conflict.

Furthermore, it would be unreasonable to anticipate that your partner will always be complimentary. After all, you two are thinking about getting married. And wouldn't it be wonderful if he talked to you about a habit or quality of yours that bothered him? True, receiving criticism hurts. (12:11 in Hebrews) However, it is not abusive speech if it is spoken out of love and with good intentions. Proverbs 27:6

But screaming, slapping, punching, or reviling are very other things. Scripture forbids "wrath, anger, evil behaviour , and abusive words." (See Col. 3:8) When someone uses their "power" to degrade, threaten, or oppress others, Jehovah is indignant. (4:1; 8:9 in Ecclesiastes). No man has ever despised his own body; instead, he feeds and cherishes it, according to God's Word, which instructs husbands to "be loving their wives as their own bodies." In Ephesians 5:28 and 29, A man who treats the lady he is courting unfairly or uses abusive language makes it clear that he is unsuitable for marriage. He simultaneously provokes the wrath of Jehovah God himself!

You're Not to Blame!

However, abusers frequently place the blame on their victims. Therefore, it's possible that occasionally you think it's your fault that your lover becomes so upset. His rage, though, might not even be particularly related to you. Many times, violent guys grew up in homes where using violence or using abusive language was commonplace. d Young males in some countries are impacted by the dominant culture, where men are expected to be in charge. A young man may experience peer pressure to act masculine. He can feel threatened by whatever you say or do because of his lack of confidence.

No matter what, you are not to blame for someone else's outbursts. Violence and abusive language are never acceptable

Adapting Your Thoughts

However, you might need to change how you see things. How so? Well, if a female has grown up surrounded by violence and hurtful speech, she may perceive abuse as usual. She might put up with such unchristian behaviour instead of recoiling from it—possibly even finding it appealing. Yes, some abuse victims say they become tired of males who are overly kind. Some teenage girls harbor the delusion that they can alter their lover.

You must "be converted by making your mind over" if any of this applies to you. (Rom. 12:2) You need to take Jehovah's perspective on the abusive behaviour to heart and perceive it as disgusting through prayer, study, and meditation. Realize that you don't deserve to be treated unfairly. Realizing that you cannot influence an angry boyfriend can help you cultivate modesty—a feeling of your limitations. He must alter; it is his duty to do so! in Galatians 6:5.

In certain circumstances, young women suffer abuse as a result of having a low sense of value. I cannot picture life without him, and I cannot imagine finding someone better, says Kathrin, who was introduced at the beginning. Similar to Helga, a young woman, "I let him hit me because it's still better than not being acknowledged at all," she stated of her partner.

Do these perspectives seem like a solid basis for a fulfilling relationship? If you can't even love yourself, how can you possibly love someone else? (19:19 in Matthew) Develop a healthy sense of self-respect. e Suffering abuse won't assist you in accomplishing that. Abuse may "strip you of all your self-esteem," as a young woman by the name of Irena is aware from personal experience.

Accepting Reality

Some people might find it difficult to admit that their relationship is toxic, especially if strong romantic sentiments have grown. But keep your eyes open to the reality. According to a proverb from the Bible, "Shrewd is he who sees the disaster and goes on to disguise himself, while the inexperienced have passed along and must pay the price." in Proverbs 22:3 "When you fall in love with the guy, you are as good as blind and you perceive only his wonderful features," a young woman named Hanna recalled. But if you are being mistreated, it's critical that you recognize him for what he is. And if your lover ever acts threatening or demeaning toward you, something is very wrong. Try not to rationalize him, rationalize your feelings, or assign blame. Abuse will only become worse if it goes unaddressed, according to experience. Your health could be at grave danger!

Naturally, it would be preferable to avoid interacting with someone who lacks self-control. Prophecy 22:24 As a result, it is wise to learn more about a potential date if you do not know him well. Why not advise that you get to know one another in a group setting at first? By doing this, you can get to know him without falling in love right away. Inquire further by asking: Who are his friends? What genres of sports, movies, video games, and music does he enjoy? Does he express any interest in spiritual matters in his conversation? Speak to his acquaintances, such as the elders of his local congregation. They'll let you know if his mature and godly behaviour has earned him the reputation of being "well reported on" by others. —Acts 16:2.

Several Red Flags

He frequently makes disparaging statements about you, your loved ones, or your pals, whether you're by yourself or around others.

He typically disregards your desires or sentiments

He demands to always be aware of your locations and make all decisions for you in an effort to manage every element of your life

He shouts at you, shoves you, or makes threats.

He attempts to persuade you to show unsuitable signs of affection

You hardly ever do anything without considering whether it would annoy him in some manner.